Hands

Hands

Tiziana & Gianni Baldizzone
Boris Cyrulnik

Translated from the French
by
Katia & Ken Holmes

Contents

Introduction

by

TIZIANA & GIANNI BALDIZZONE

MUCH OF OUR LIVES have been dedicated to travel and photography, to portraying what was foreign, exotic or inaccessible. At least so we thought. Then one day, while sorting out photos — taken over a period of more than twenty years, we realised that, unwittingly, we had also been trying to shed light on our own lives. The different realities in the images we had brought back from far-flung corners of the planet served primarily to illuminate the ambiguities and obscurities of our own little world — a world we could not see clearly because we were too close to it.

This is just one of the things we learned in putting together this book, which seemed to suggest itself to us — something that had never occurred to us while out in the field. Reviewing several thousand pictures, as we did, brought back memories of many wonders, and of intense exhaustion. We relived the strange sensation that used to strike us so vividly every time we got home: the feeling that we had left behind us *another body* — in Tibet, in Sumatra, in the Mauritanian Hodh — *another body* which somehow suited us better. Rediscovering on paper or on screen the vitality in those faces, those silhouettes from so far away, reinforced the idea that what the West has gained in comfort, in health and in safety has been won at the expense of the simple freedom of our bodies. We live to a riper old age, we eat better food, we strain our muscles less than our counterparts in Africa or Asia, but our bodies and our gestures reveal an inhibition, a constraint, not consistent with living life to the full. Exhibiting our bodies on the beach in summer seems unlikely to change this, despite the compensation we seem to find in it. Our return to Europe, as we put back on our post-modern citizen's body, had always been accompanied by a feeling of loss, despite the pleasures of sitting at our own table, laden with longed-for treats. This change of body, which was necessary in order to reconcile ourselves with so-called civilised life, meant abdicating an ancient freedom, which had become natural to us too while we were away. More than that, it meant cutting ourselves off from some primeval form of beauty. The proof of this soon emerged from our "image-box", ruthless as ever. All

7

photographers-cum-travellers will tell you that, while it is very difficult to capture the beauty of bodies encountered in a milieu as sophisticated as ours, there is rarely a withered or lame old man, standing in front of his hut in the Sahel or seated in a Chennai market, whose body does not emit beauty, or even splendour.

We had this nagging feeling: *over there*, the first body you meet has spirit, even when it carries the stigma of physical trials, illness, or even destitution. This feeling was followed by another, just as compelling: modern flesh, enhanced by the costly cosmetic of progress, has lost not only its animal naivety and its innocence, but also its grace; one is tempted to say *its soul*.

As we were reviewing all the men and women we had captured going about their daily lives in another world, the suspicion grew that we Westerners are in the process of losing yet another thing — the gift of existing *through our hands*. How many photographs of hands we had snapped, observed, admired; hands adorned or sullied, busy or at rest, sorrowful or joyful! As they danced their ballet, they seemed to be whispering this strange secret: "Perhaps you are forgetting that we made you what you are."

No more prompting was necessary. This book was a must. And what is true of our hands is equally true of our bodies. Humans began by off-loading heavy manual work and complex tasks onto machines, which was fine, but there was a price to pay. The price, as usual, can only be calculated after the event: our hands have become idle but, above all, deprived of direct contact with the stuff of reality, they are gradually losing their inventiveness and their genius. Even their beauty is no longer what it was — manicurists who still know how to use their own smooth and faultless fingers have doubtless contributed to this. Our hands have become at best some sort of abstract sketch, terribly lacking in character.

Having had to give up their leading role on the stage of our personal theatre, hands have lost a great deal of their *eloquence*. This is a quality which comes from way back (as Boris Cyrulnik, who kindly took an interest in our work, explains in the next section). The capacity of hands for expression is only rivalled by that of speech, which is usually credited, a little unfairly, with the monopoly. The advantage of the language of hands is that, apart from a few local expressions, it is universal and needs no translation.

Of course we Latins know how to let our hands speak — even when it would be better for them to be silent. But our hands are less and less animated by the need to *do* things, and therefore play a less significant part in spinning the web of symbolism which surrounds the things humans consider important (as the six chapters of this book show). So today, hands have less and less to tell us, less to accomplish, and less skill in doing it.

By acquiring ever-increasing power through machines, have so-called civilised humans been dispossessed of their best and most valuable asset? In losing the use of our hands, have we lost our touch? When Boris Cyrulnik put our concerns into context, we saw the truth of this. It is to their hands and feet that men and women owe their existence as human beings for over a million years, and probably for a lot longer. In all that time, humans have never stopped inventing cunning new ways to enhance the dexterity of their fingers and the mobility of their legs. No doubt they have paid a price for this at each stage in their development (progress never fails to take its toll), but the history of the species as a whole shows that, so far at least, the cost has not been too high and the progress achieved indisputable. Let us hope that humanity continues to maintain a wise balance.

This is the message conveyed to us, wordlessly, by the hands of these men, women and children, the hands of the anonymous characters who have been invited to "talk" in this book. Though not philosophers, they remind us of the risk of becoming impoverished by forgetting what our bodies can do and can tell us. If we try to fly too close to the sun, we may fall back to earth with a jolt.

AUTOBIOGRAPHY
OF MY HANDS

by

Boris Cyrulnik

I MUST HAVE BEEN six years old and already quite a walker when one day, while out with a doggy chum, I decided to start walking on all fours, as he did, so as not to offend him. That is how I discovered the impossibility of doing *as he did*, since it was too uncomfortable for me to walk on the only pads I had — those of the soles of my feet and the palms of my hands — and also very painful for me to walk on my knees. This difficult choice became the starting point of my intellectual journey. I decided to embark upon a discovery of my hands.

My first discovery was that I belonged to the sole species endowed with *hands* and I was probably therefore not of the same family as animals. Maybe I was even "destined to have dominion over the fish of the sea, and over the birds of the air, and over the cattle, and over all the earth, and over every creeping thing that creeps upon the earth," as it says in Genesis. The fact of having hands and not paws must signify something, surely? In my child's mind, every event took on meaning, especially when something unusual caught my attention.

Some time later, I learnt by chance that, even if the fact of having hands classed me among supernatural living beings, some small space needed to be left alongside me for larger primates, so clever at picking fruit, and especially orang-outangs, right-handed like myself. Fortunately for my theory, monkeys have four hands, making them quadrumanes. This quantity of hands devaluing them somewhat, I remained alone in possessing the very precious privilege of having *two* feet to tread the earth and *two* hands to raise me to the heavens.

In order to clarify the origin of this peculiarity, I needed to set out and discover my hands' prehistory. It was thus I realised that it all started under water.

Once upon a time, three hundred million years ago, there was a group of vertebrates that one would classify today as "fish". Their pectoral fin was a sort of humerus stuck onto the chest and accompanied by two other bones, that one could consider as a radius and an ulna, inconveniently prolonged away from the body by seven bones which could correspond to my fingers!

Fish behind my origins! It was all very well them explaining to me that frogs, birds and all mammals have bones equivalent to those of an arm or a hand; I would not have it. A paw is not a hand!

Indonesia, 2001.
Our feet and our hands:
the most "human"
parts of the body.

When it was discovered that five or six million years ago Mr Australopithecus lived in Ethiopia, with his wife, Mrs Lucy, it had to be noted that they had hands. That changes everything, because, once one has hands, one does things with them. One can even make them do more or less anything. Having hands enables action both in the material world, by making tools of worked flint, and in the world of expression, by making hand gestures. Humankind's technological and literary adventure started the day when humans — or their ancestors — realised just that. The hand as communicator-toolmaker was born. Its gestation had lasted several million years.

Human hands have been on vacation ever since the moment human beings stood upright to walk, swinging the pelvis forward and hollowing the lower back. Their hands might have atrophied, as happened with the kangaroo, or spread out to push against the air, as did the birds', or hardened, like those of moles, to rummage through the earth, or become sharper, like those of the dolphin, to slice through water. Humankind opted for a different strategy: it took advantage of the holiday, naturally provided by being two-footed, to beat the air. This unexpected freedom enabled humans to use their hands to make tools — and linguistic signals. Now become a communicator-toolmaker, the hand was to set in motion the whole of my cultural adventure.

Mr and Mrs Sapiens were already creating masterpieces even during the time when they were making badly-cut tools and unfinished mechanical objects. On simple pebbles or dried animal bones, they drew the world as they viewed it. The hand which enabled them to make an as-yet imperfect tool made it possible to project their world onto the screen formed by the smooth surface of a stone or a flat bone. Their personal world became visible. Thanks to their manual skill, they fashioned at will a world that they were now capable of "predicting". They already saw themselves as masters of the world! And the discovery of fire did not make things any better, since by rubbing two sticks together or by banging one round flint against another, they brought to life a mysterious energy source, the power of which they could harness.

That was the first metamorphosis of the human condition. Humans were no longer slaves of immediate circumstances; thanks to their hands, they could master the world and organise existence. Mr and Mrs Neanderthal, the first Europeans, with their short thumbs and long little fingers, had certainly set up schools where one could learn to carve stone and make knives and sharp instruments. The simple fact of "visualising" the shape of a knife or scraper and then being able to give that form to the shapeless stones they held in their hands was proof already of their intellectual capacity for abstract thought. This marvellous and terrible faculty made them able to form representations of death; the absolute abstraction. As this gift no doubt drove them mad with anguish, they had then to fight off their terror. Hence they built tombs and decorated them in an attempt to control the notions they had of death. Humankind was, in a certain way, forced into artistic creation to fight off fear of the void and the infinity of death that their intelligence had ended up making palpable to them. What a marvellous price to pay for fighting off anxiety!

This personal necessity for artistic representation gave birth to notions of beauty, and hence ugliness, as well as morality, hence immorality, and of resemblance and dissimilarity. The coloured stones placed around the body of someone just dead — but still alive in the relatives' minds — became metamorphised stones; semantic stones which meant, "We are no longer stones because, coloured and placed as a crown around the dead person, we now delineate the body and make him or her still live figuratively in others' thoughts. Thanks to us, the person is a little less dead and those who loved that person will not yet have abandoned his or her body." Thus speak pebbles once transformed into a work of art. Less worried, thanks to this funeral rite which kept the departed alive a little longer, and less ashamed, simply through not having abandoned the body of the one they loved, the dead person's close relatives felt reassured and "moral" and accepted with more ease the idea of carrying on life without him or her.

The gestures of the people of one hundred thousand years ago painted stones, laid them out around the corpse and scattered flowers upon it. The skill of these gestures enabled them to avoid submission to the demands of the immediate present, thus escaping the real situation by preferring obedience to the representations they had just invented. In brief, they chose to liberate themselves from reality by chaining themselves to symbols.

That is how they came to engrave drawings resembling the hunted animal on the bone launchers used for hurling stones at far-off game. Their manual dexterity was a "magic" enabling them to influence reality. The drawn deer on the bone assegai spear was going to penetrate the body of the real deer it resembled. Controlling the distress of death, through the use of tomb art and technique, and bringing about death using "magically" decorated assegai were things that allowed the world of transcendence to be inhabited for good.

The hand, giving form to our thoughts, modified the real and became the tool for making representations. We could, from that moment on, let the imagination go wild. The Bible awarded the right hand the moral and aesthetic qualities which had set the world in order whereas the left hand saw itself attributed clumsiness, shame, blemish, treason and all that pins us to the earth.

This share-out of the world carries through to the heavens, where the chosen sit at the right hand of God whereas the reprobate have to put up with being to the left. The Qur'an too puts the virtuous to Allah's right and the lost to the left, following, after death, the world categorisation started in life. Right and virtue will forever oppose what is "sinister" and gauche.

And yet, it is the left hemisphere which controls both speech and the right hand. Something real is much more ambiguous than its abstract representation, itself at least straightforward. Only ideas are ideal: reality forces us into compromises, which are, by the way, rarely as glorious or as shameful as the notions of the right and the sinister. That is why the right hand regularly accompanies speech coming from the left... the seat of the soul.

The hand takes part in speech, which it accompanies viscerally and spiritually, as is shown in an exemplary way by the photos Tiziana and Gianni Baldizzone have gathered together in this book. These photos are all worthy subjects of meditation if one really wants to know what being man or woman implies and what speaking means.

When I give a talk, my hands set the tempo of my speech, beating the rhythm of the words as they organise its melody. When a word happens to fail me, they compensate for the blank, filling it by sketching some gesture to signify the missing object. It is not uncommon for my hands to draw the shape of my ideas, miming for example the shape of a roof, my cheek on a pillow or my well-fed stomach. They may even become quasi-words, when they draw in space arbitrary gestures which everyone can "hear". The fact of moving our hands in conventional ways fashions a world of words even more evident than the one created by wagging the tongue.

Our hands take part in our speech even when we think we are only speaking with the mouth. Even more troubling is the fact that they also participate in the manner our words adopt to illuminate the world. Many writers explain that they think with their hands, as it is only in *the act of writing* that they manage to give form to their ideas. The way in which I think and express myself is not the same when I type on a keyboard, when

On the steps leading to the mosque at Batipuah, in Minangkabao (western Sumatra, 2001). Our hands "speak" even when not moving: no other part of the body, except the face, is charged with such expressivity.

I take pen to hand, when I talk to someone or when I dive inside myself using my inner language. As the impulse given to the intellectual, manual and verbal adventure comes from the left side of the brain, whereas the right looks after syntheses, I wonder whether asymmetry is not a necessary thing for the construction of the world. Chemical molecules are asymmetrical, matter is asymmetrical, just as are the hemispheres of the brain and probably even the sexes. What would happen were our hands symmetrical, with right and left equal in both handling matter and making mental representations? Probably life would not exist, as it results from movements tending to balance two asymmetrical forces. The balance of molecules, hemispheres and ideas is only perfect in death. Life, however, is a struggle to tame the imbalance necessary for life. If our two hands were equal, our ideas would be too. The result would be a world brought to a halt — a monotonous world, without surprise, without event and without conflict: a non-life preceding death.

As I write this, my hand makes me understand that this perhaps

explains why animals have a poorer mental life than us: they are not one-sided! Their left paws are as good as their right paws. They do have a mental life — made of sensorial representations, odours, images and sounds — since they are endowed with memory allowing them to adapt and to learn to resolve the problems posed by the habitat in which they must live. But that is just the point: their mental life is solely a response to their habitat problems whereas ours is infinitely richer... since we must argue and suffer incessantly, in order to resolve the problems that we ourselves *invent*. To do that, we need to combine consciousness, so as the more easily to resolve the problems we continually create and that those like us constantly let loose upon us. These are problems which simply would not exist if we did not have consciousness. I believe this difficulty, this very suffering, to be a good thing because it gives purpose to our lives. It forces us to meet and confront each other, to invent codes of behaviour... and it makes our hands transcribe our thoughts, good or bad but definitely wondrous.

Now we understand why Mr and Mrs Neanderthal had much larger bones in the right arm than in the left. They used their right arms more,

thereby proving that, in their skulls, the left hemisphere was larger than its counterpart and capable of inventing words which could intrigue, create interest and cause suffering.

The cult of the hand could thus begin. Forty thousand years ago, some humans knew how to draw hands on cave walls. In so doing they created one of the first art exhibitions and one which was the most universal of all, as each of us, without exception, can identify with it. Why hands? Why that particular fashion; that style of painting, without frontier, found wherever there were humans? Furthermore, these paleo-taggers used modern production methods. They placed one hand, fingers splayed, against the rock wall while the other hand threw red and black colours around it. Taking the hand away, they discovered on the rock the negative outline of the left hand. They were already right-handed, forty thousand years ago.

Whole cave walls are thus covered with the most striking left hands. A large number of these hands have a phalanx missing; sometimes four. These missing finger parts are found tagged elsewhere on the same rock face. Archaeo-detectives pondering this mystery have come up with quite different conclusions. Those of religious bent claim that this is to do with ritual sacrifices, proving that sacred mutilations were an uncontrolled affair until religion civilised them. Researchers keener on justice think this is more a case of the guilty being punished for paleo-offences deserving one or four fingers to be amputated. Others, trained in linguistics, think they can decipher through these images a hand code in which the finger positions refer to some concept which was probably metaphysical. As for myself, I think the latter argument the most likely to convince me; ever since humans have been humans (experts date this between fifty thousand and six million years ago) they have spoken using their hands and they have made their hands talk. The photographs gathered here show that well enough. Incidentally, this fits well with today's neurological science, which states that stimulation of the left brain provokes at one and the same time a flow of words and movements in the right hand. It is also in line with linguistic theories explaining that when two humans collaborate to agree upon a signal, they create a new world, upsetting the old values in the process. Hands can send signals, just as much as the coloured stones laid out in a tomb and just as much as the clothes and jewellery which make their wearers distinctive, accompany celebrations or mourning or designate a specific function or social class.

That is why, since the Roman era, school was not intended to teach useful knowledge but to *classify* those who would become grown-up humans, by teaching them to spot and decode a multitude of distinctive signals. After a few years of good education, these young people could recognise each other by the slightest gesture, the slightest inflexion of the voice, and take their place, knowingly, in the category to which they belonged; that of the fine, distinguished mind or that of the rustic mind

Walata, southern Mauritania, 1999. Once a year, the fronts of the houses, decorated with coloured "protective" designs, are repainted. This task is assigned to the women, as is everything to do with the household. Everywhere, the hand is the guardian of symbols invented by the mind.

easy to dominate. Rhetoric also had a social function. It not only presided over the ordering of words, which had to be made as persuasive as possible, but also over a whole world of gesture, intended to be eloquent in itself and created by posture, hand movements and especially finger movements. Each social group thus defined its own behavioural code, specifying how one must act at table... and all the hand movements that one was supposed to use to assert oneself to others and to occupy the finest place in society. The necessary knowledge was acquired in the field but training in these gestures of mutual recognition, between the well-born, was only learnt at school.

It is a strange mistake to believe that the point of school is to acquire practical knowledge. It is in life itself that one learns to live. At school, one is rather learning signals; verbal or gestural routines and the behavioural rituals which enable each person to stand out and make statements about whatever set they belong to.

The Peul Bororo people (Niger):
a boy caught by surprise
at the camp edge (1984).
Opposite: a young girl to be married
decked out for the premarital
celebrations during which the boys
of the group will offer themselves
to be chosen by their future bride (1999).
In either case, the hand takes part
in the rhetoric of feelings.

Thus is the hand's symbolising power. The human body is more or less the same today as it was at the time of the Cro-Magnon. A man's body, however, is very different from that of a woman and one may well wonder what is the point of such a difference, as species exist where male and female are extremely hard to differentiate, yet this in no way prevents them from reproducing.

Among the innumerable characteristics of the human species, one is of particular importance for our hands: the one that orders us to walk on our feet! In a still recent time, when human relationships could not take place without a physical meeting, people first used their legs to travel and then set their bodies facing each other, in a posture and at a distance which enabled the proper use of speech. Then each party got on with the business of evoking their inner world and making known their wishes and their will. Today, this scenario has been somewhat modified by technology. Yet when one wishes to have a real, sensorial, emotional and verbal contact with another person, one must position the body adequately and prepare it for the contact to come; at this time any part of the body can send a signal. One cannot just approach the other any old how. Before speaking, precise mechanisms need to be brought into play, with a whole behavioural syntax. First the gaze while approaching: people must look at each other but not stare; that would be indecent. And then the smiles, to show a friendly disposition. The gaze itself looks for contact, to let it be known that the other has been seen, that the other already exists in one's own soul. This is quickly followed by a hand gesture which announces what will be said: affection, threat... whatever. From afar, the palm can have a symbolism analogous to that of other physical signs of openness — the open mouth of a smile, open arms to show hospitality, raised brows permitting wide-open eyes to show surprise. Likewise but with a hundred nuances, the declensions of the palm express all modes of welcome.

Since the hand is a cousin of the tongue, it is not surprising that finger symbolism has its own real alphabet.

The thumb is a finger apart; shorter, more robust and often considered master of fingers. In Salian law, the scale of mutilation for offences stipulates that a thumb is worth half a hand. This digit is said to bear moral values, hence it is sometimes made to bear a ring with noble attributes, such as those worn by the Bambara chiefs or by our bishops of old when they were not officiating.

In the Roman Catholic church, priests use their thumbs to consecrate the faithful during baptisms and confirmations. In the beginnings of Christianity, it was the only digit allowed to make the sign of the cross. For Shiite and Sunni Muslims, the thumb represents the Prophet and the other fingers his companions. Sculptors and painters always put Christ's thumb inside his palms, as though it might be impertinent to see it stand by itself, distanced from the other fingers.

André Carénini, an anthropologist of the thumb, explains that this finger often represents virility. In India, the betrothed should hold her intended's thumb, if she wants a boy. If she holds all the fingers except the thumb, she will have a girl. A common expression of friendly virility in our Western culture is the "thumbs up" sign of the American GI, signifying *good luck*. The French are not exactly making a hand-language mistranslation when they use the same gesture to signify *this person is great*. Trappist monks used it to designate their prior, like the Japanese who use it to speak of their boss. In films about gladiators, when the crowd held their thumbs up, the gesture signified, "Let the vanquished die." In this case, the meaning was close to that implied when one draws the thumb from ear to ear beneath the jaw, to represent the throat being cut. Those in the crowd who wished the fighters to be spared showed a fist closed over the thumb — Hollywood has mistranslated Juvenal here and made a

In the streets of a village
of Minangkabao
(western Sumatra, 2001).
The thumb, digit of power,
can also express affection.

nonsense by asking the actors to point their thumbs down to petition death.

Only French children still say, "Thumb, I'm not playing any more." To express the same thing, Germans put their palms forwards and the English use their arms to mimic the gesture of cutting.

It seems that in Sparta, teachers bit the thumb of a child to be punished, as in the Middle Ages in France when the lady of the house would bite maidservants who displeased her. These methods of education are less in use today yet vestiges of such an attitude remain in Sicily, where furious people bite their thumbs and throw the "bite" in the direction of the person who is the object of their ill-will.

The meanings of gestures evolve just like those of words, as both cases involve living organisms.

Social discourse can even use the thumb to express a metaphysical message. The "fig" gesture is a fine example. Put your thumb in between the index and middle fingers and then look at the figure this creates. It makes you think straightaway of a female sexual organ, with the thumb representing the turgescent clitoris between the two lips. This gesture has been quoted by the greatest names in mythological literature; the sort of literature one talks about to seem learned but never really reads. André Carénini writes that Aristophanes makes allusion to this gesture in his comedies, four centuries before Christ. Ovid talked of it as an "obscene hand" and Dante used it as an insult to the Creator, since along all the Mediterranean coast, in Provence as in Crete, someone who wanted ill to fall on a person denounced that person as a "fig thief". The Templars, during their trials, were accused of having "figged the Pope" and this enchanted Rabelais, who straightaway invented the term "Popefig" — certainly making him worthy of being burnt at the stake. The very Catholic poet of our time, Paul Claudel, even went as far as appropriating the expression which, however, went out of fashion after him. This obscene thumb gesture has survived in Italy and southern Spain, where it is used by children to ward off the evil eye, whereas in Turkey and Greece it remains an insult. As is the case with all language, hand talk may give rise to all sorts of partial or total mis-interpretations or lead to misunderstandings or even cause tragedies, if one does not take care to avoid language traps.

A hand can bless or offend, depending upon the movement it is ordered to make, just as a tongue can enchant or humiliate according to the sounds it has to modulate. The hand can even replace the sacred figure not allowed to be represented. On the mosaic of Isaac's sacrifice, at San-Vitale in Ravenna, it is a hand which descends from heaven to represent an unportrayable God. At Saint-Appolinaire-in-Classe, it is God's voice which indicates, through his hand, the transfiguration of the cross which saves the world.

Thus, if a hand can take the place of God, it is logical that, like God, it can bear stigmata, the miraculous marks found on the body in the places where Christ suffered his five wounds. Yet, for human hands to represent Christ's expiation and, through that, the redemption of our sins, their own-ers must be pious indeed and have palms, considered as identical with Christ's own, which can show, either spontaneously or on request, the vas-cular syndrome of an authentic wound, that really bleeds, scars, re-opens and bleeds yet again. Over seven centuries, from Saint Francis of Assisi to Padre Pio, the Christian West has made hands bleed, thereby showing tremendous identification with the hands of the one who suffered for his fellow humans.

The index finger has a curious history. It plays a part in the development of all our children, assuming an important relational meaning from very early on. Since the invention of ultrasound scans, it has been easy to observe how, towards the end of pregnancy, when the mother is speaking,

Marriage in Chennai, South India, 2000. The mother of the betrothed places on her daughter's forehead the *tikha*, the "third eye" which is supposed to enable the mind to see beyond mere appearances. This gesture is considered to have the highest blessing.

A little boy of the Peul Bororo people (Niger, 1999). He is taking advantage of his parents' backs being turned to drain the remains of a glass of tea, in secret. The hand and the mouth: the first investigatory tools in our discovery of the world.

the baby responds with accelerated heartbeat, by jiggling around and by groping for whatever "floating objects" it needs to identify around it. As soon as it manages to seize the umbilical cord, or else its own thumb or the other hand, it brings the "object" to its mouth which, at this stage of its development, is quite an efficient way of identifying things. Reassured by this method of getting to know both itself and its environment, the little one's heart slows and, pacified, waits for the next event. In fact, what really counts for the foetus is not the content of the mother's speech but its sensory quality. If the mother says, "Daddy got a pay rise," what stimulates the child and sets off these exploratory reactions is not the figure on the pay cheque but the low frequencies of the mother's voice which come and vibrate against the parts of the infant's body equipped with tactile sensors: the mouth and the hands. Thus, when the mother speaks, she caresses, without knowing it, the mouth and hands of the child she carries; the latter, stimulated, takes advantage to explore his or her environment and learn.

After birth, infants continue this sort of apprenticeship, bringing every object they meet to their lips in order to *learn* them. Then suddenly, around the tenth month, they start pointing the index finger at objects beyond their reach. This modest hand gesture is an important thing to note, as it asserts that, by so acting, the child will speak. To think of making this indicative gesture with the index finger, one has first to have become capable of imagining the following behavioural scenario: I need that object, inaccessible for me as I am too small, but by pointing my index finger towards it, my gesture will have an effect on my mother's mental world and she will go and fetch the object and bring it to me. This indicative gesture is, clearly, a "meaningful gesture", a semiotic gesture which is preparing the meeting of two mental worlds. As we pointed out, the hand and speech are indeed very closely linked!

At that stage, culture has not yet struck. It will punish later, towards the age of four, by forbidding the child to point at something it can designate with a word. Pointing with the index finger becomes impolite with respect to the culture which, if the child still points the index finger at that age, has failed to inculcate verbal expression. This is why, in Asia, it is thought that if you do not speak well and cannot stop yourself pointing to objects, you may, if need be, use the middle finger. This shows that at least you manage to control the primitive impulse and accomplish, despite it all, a cultural action. One may indicate oneself using the index finger but one cannot point it at someone else; that would be considered bad.

What is astonishing is the universality of this feeling of discomfort. In Turkey, one can only point at objects, not people. In Israel, it is considered an evil gesture. In Central America, one points mostly with the chin but never at all with the finger. In Cameroon, it is believed that if one points to a wound or a burn with the index finger, it will suppurate. There is a highly socialised emotional power in the slightest gesture of the index finger. If you do not believe me, wag your index finger at a child and then do the same thing to your boss. In the first of the cases, you may give rise to a certain degree of intimidation but in the second be sure that you will stir up indignation which will not be without consequence.

The behavioural grammar of the index finger permits the structuring of a large number of meanings. In many countries, the index fingers of each hand set against each other, end to end, signifies conflict. To make horns of them casts an evil spell on the person towards whom the gesture is pointed. The evil index finger speaks the same language in Pompeii and Japan, in India as in Spain or in Colombia. To be behind a man and make the fun gesture of horns "decorating" his head tells everyone that he has been cuckolded. It is strange that this gesture has the same meaning in numerous cultures, yet no one really knows its origin.

As all living organisms, gestures are born, are transmitted (like the words of a language) and then disappear one day, not always to be replaced. The *pied de nez* gesture (thumb on nose and fingers wagging), which for such a long time enchanted the childhood of all the world's kids, was born in France in the sixteenth century. Rabelais' hero, Pantagruel, might have had something to do with it and France's colonial venture may have universalised this fancy gesture, which is perhaps less simple than it appears. It disappeared in a single generation, around the demonstrations of May 1968 it seems, when the broken tradition was vaguely replaced by the gesture of tapping the inflated cheek with the tip of the index finger, so as to make small doubting or mocking farts.

The middle finger does not have a good reputation. This infamous, impure, shameful digit is the vagina finger. Greeks used it to insult each other but Asiatics find it more proper to point things out with the middle

In a street of Tichitt,
eastern Mauritania, 1999.
The man, librarian of a great family,
uses a gesture to make it understood
that he is willing to be photographed...
but that it taxes his modesty.
This facial mime accentuated
by a hand gesture,
as precise as an ideogram,
is one of thousands of "characters"
of gestural writing
that the universal subconscious
has recorded and classified.

finger, which is less vexing than the index finger, according to them. Were we real scientists, we would seek a research grant to invite several Asian people to travel in Greece and we would then observe the effect their hand gestures produce in those around them.

The ring finger, less skilled sexually, therefore has a better reputation. It has been the finger for rings since Roman time. Christ and Buddha put their thumb to it to give a "metaphysical" aspect to their hand (thumb and finger make a circle).

As for the little finger, it is the finger of divination, the one which told all to the adult's ear, at the time when people believed it sufficient to block one's ears with the little fingers to awaken prophetic visions.

Strangely enough, immigrants learn the words of the language of their host country in a few years but often have a struggle to integrate the accompanying gestures. In the Olympic Games of facial mimicry, American women would be gold medalists and well-integrated Iranian or African woman will learn the same mimes quickly yet will have much more difficulty learning the hand "ballets" that are the done thing in the host country. It is as though hand gestures learnt in earliest childhood were the hardest to change since they are the most strongly imprinted in the bodily memory. People who learnt to hold up the little finger while downing their cup of tea, so as to appear delicate, will keep the habit until the end of their days. The cultural context, which changed so much in France in 1968, attributed to this raised little finger an affectation which needed to be challenged. Thus it was the children of the "sixty-eighters" who, having learnt to raise their cups with a closed fist, put an end to this mannerism inherited from another time.

However, cultural integration of the hand has been easy in the case of jewellery. Skeletons with bejewelled hands have been found in prehistoric shelters. Etruscan and Scythian rings are still beautiful today. Phoenician women coloured their lips, nipples and nails with the same red as our

beauties of the twenty-first century. The colours found in Nefertiti's make-up box would still be acceptable to modern-day women, even though the latter are served by all the refinements of today's technical society.

From the manipulating hand which we share with larger primates, through the hand which grips between thumb and forefinger up to the semantic hand, which "speaks" and tells of our individual or social history, one finds a constant spectrum of actions and meanings. It is more or less impossible to move the hand without it meaning something. Those with total hearing loss cannot learn to reproduce sounds but, since they can see, learn to sign with their hands. If a few such people live together, it will be enough for them to invent a gestural language — American, French, Danish, Chinese or Aboriginal — that is perfectly efficient. Each people has its own hand language, since it is all about gestural conventions linked to their culture.

Thus can a hand either grip or think according to the intimate intentions of each person's inner world. The way in which a culture invites us to use our hands therefore reveals, to those who know how to see it, the very structures of the body social. That is what Tiziana and Gianni Baldizzone have seen so well. They are not satisfied, in this book, with just *showing* the hands of the world, they make them *speak*, and thereby teach us far more than any supposedly knowledgeable discourses about the condition of the social world (that of traditional cultures mostly but also, through the tacit comparisons which they cannot help evoking, that of our own). This is because their work is situated not just in space but also in time, at a crucial moment in history.

When civilisation's main activity was making flint tools for warding off animals or scraping hides, the hand needed a skilful and strong grip to be able to execute what thought foresaw. Immediately after that, in the following two million years, the invention of a multitude of tools (and then machines) extended the hands' effect and came between the forearm's muscle power and the object to be worked on. The more machines were invented, the more muscular energy diminished. Each technological discovery has changed the way in which we use our hands and think of the human condition. Not only did the invention of the iron ploughshare in the eleventh century relieve the labourer's back and forearm of quite a few wicked pains, it also reduced the infant mortality rate. Digging the earth better yet with less effort, it made for better harvests and small children could eat their fill. The weaving loom becoming mechanised in the nineteenth century turned upside down the way in which society was conceived, relativising the value of body weight and the power of the hand. The machine-aided motor gesture brought about both an increase in its ability to mould reality and a liberation of a new energy source for us: thought.

Humanity has gained victory over its natural condition by making the hand the most skilful servant of its thought. However, there is no progress without side effects and we should not allow this gain to cost us too dear.

26

Hand of a weaver-woman: the use of a bamboo loom was already known in prehistoric times (Arunachal Pradesh, north-east India, 1990). A gesture of elevated and very ancient know-how, soon fated to disappear.

The reader curious to know more may well wish to consult the following (fascinating) works which were my companions for this text. Here is the list, even though it could contain many others:

Concerning the evolutionary process which helped shape our bodies, particularly the hand: Jean Piveteau, La Main et l'hominisation, *Paris, Éditions Masson, 1991.*

Concerning funeral rites and our way of taming death: André Leroi-Gourhan, Le Geste et la Parole, *Paris, Éditions Albin Michel, 1965.*

On the relationship religions have with "right" and "left": Desmond Morris, Magie du corps, *Paris, Éditions Bernard Grasset, 1986.*

On the mystery of brain hemispheres and their influence on our gestures: Pierre Feyereisen, Le Cerveau et la communication, *Paris, Presses Universitaires de France, 1994.*

On the mystery of speech: Roger Saban, Aux sources du langage articulé, *Paris, Éditions Masson, 1993.*

On language's ability to create symbols: John R. Searle, Les Actes du langage (essai de philosophie du langage), *Paris, Éditions Hermann, 1972.*

On the operative function of gesture: John Langshaw Austin, Quand dire c'est faire, *Paris, Éditions du Seuil, 1970.*

On the singular destiny of each of our fingers: André Carénini, "La symbolique manuelle," in Jean Poirier, Histoire des mœurs *(vol. 2, Modes et Modèles), Paris, Éditions Gallimard, Bibliothèque de la Pléiade, 1991.*

On the different ways we have of "speaking" (with the mouth, the hands or all the body): Serge Santi Isabelle, Guaïtella, Christian Cavé, Gabrielle Konopczynski, Oralité et Gestualité (communication multimodèle, interaction), *Paris, Éditions de l'Harmattan, 1998.*

About the universality of feelings and signs which represent them: Jean-Jacques Boutaud, Sémiotique et Communication, *Paris, Éditions de l'Harmattan, 1998.*

About the singular destiny our gestures commit us to: Dominique Lestel, Paroles de singes, *Paris, Éditions de la Découverte, 1995.*

On the hearing-impaired and the way they make their hands talk: Oliver Sacks: Des yeux pour entendre: voyage aux pays des sourds, *Paris, Éditions de Seuil, 1990.*

On the way our most private intentions govern our hands: Jacques Cosnier and Catherine Kerbrat-Orrechioni, Décrire la conversation, *Presses Universitaires de Lyon, 1987.*

Hands
of
Pleasure

IT GOES WITHOUT SAYING that the hands and the face are the two places of the body where the ambivalence of our nature expresses itself the most: the mouth is nurturing and animal but it also speaks. Fingers are predatory but also knead matter and invent forms. In these zones of hyper-sensitive contact, two forces that control the destiny of the species confront each other: necessity and freedom. Being human must also have meant, in the beginnings of consciousness, living the instant when a new will drove the first man or woman to seek pleasures beyond the simple objectives assigned to living beings (satisfying hunger and procreating). Consciousness was an exacting force which soon decided upon its weapons: let mouth and fingers stop simply serving my basic needs — let them taste, try out, compare and choose... and let them manage this in such a way that, by the end of all their little tricks, the best turns out even better.

Wherever we have travelled, ceremonial traditions have tried to accom-modate this hedonistic dimension of the human adventure, with banquets and libations but also with ritual kisses, for the mouth, and ornaments, unguents and gestures of complicity or exchange, for the hand — not forgetting the signs and symbols through which one consecrates and pro-tects these privileged areas of the body which pass for thresholds of the soul.

Previous pages (28-29):
Ritual hand gestures accompanying a marriage dance (Sumatra, 2001). The hand and foot movements of the professional dancer hired for the occasion follow a grammar of emotions known by all present.

Opposite:
At a drinking fountain in a small village of the Susa Valley (Piedmont, 2002). The first cup humans ever invented...

Following pages 32-33:
A boy and a girl playing at splashing each other, during the ritual Bathing Festival, on the banks of the Tsangpo (Upper Brahmaputra), eastern Tibet, 1995. This universal play, with the hands, paves the way for later life, when other games and other pleasures will be shared.

Opposite:

Washing the groom-to-be, on the eve of a marriage: Rajasthan (north-west India), 1998.

In the villages, where people are far from rolling in money, all youngsters to be married in the year wed on the same day. Everyone seems to get something out of it: the festivities should be memorable (with nothing spared to celebrate such an event) yet without causing the financial ruin of each family concerned.

Here, the women of the young man's family are starting the beauty session. The candidate is undressed, thoroughly washed and massaged, then embalmed from head to toe with perfumed unguent. The small pot contains tamarisk powder, which has the property of making the skin soft and shiny. These ladies, whose expert hand movements pass over the future groom, laugh, thinking of the pleasure his wife will soon enjoy when caressing this body promised to her.

Following pages 36-37:

Sharing-out and preparation of betel in a Sumatran village, Indonesia (2001).

Chewing betel (a tonic which makes the equatorial humidity a little more bearable) is the pastime of both men and women in these parts. The fibres, seasoned with a powder based on areca nut, are rolled in a fresh leaf. Preparing the betel with one's own hand is obviously not a negligible part of the pleasure found in its intake.

Page 38:

The smoker's rest: on board a boat serving the banks of Lake Toba (northern Sumatra, 2001). Smelling the tobacco burning slowly between one's fingers is almost to smoke it by anticipation... Every smoker will tell you: the hand *needs* the cigarette no less than the lips.

Page 39:

Siesta time for the Peul Bororo people (Niger, 1999).

The hand as pillow, the hand as fan, the hand as fly-brush... The joy of rest after a night spent dancing or in flirtatious chat during the Worso festival, in which the boys of the group, made-up and dressed-up, are picked "on trial" by the girls.

Page 40:

Chillum-smoker in Rajasthan (1989). This pipe sometimes has a ritual function: inside it is put local tobacco but also all sorts of plants, the scents of which are considered pleasing to heaven. Hand, nose and mouth: three old accomplices...

Page 41:

The hand of an *awalay* player, in a street of Walata (southern Mauritania, 1999). One has to move the pawns (grains), from one square to the next, according to precise rules. The winning hand reveals the soul of the player.

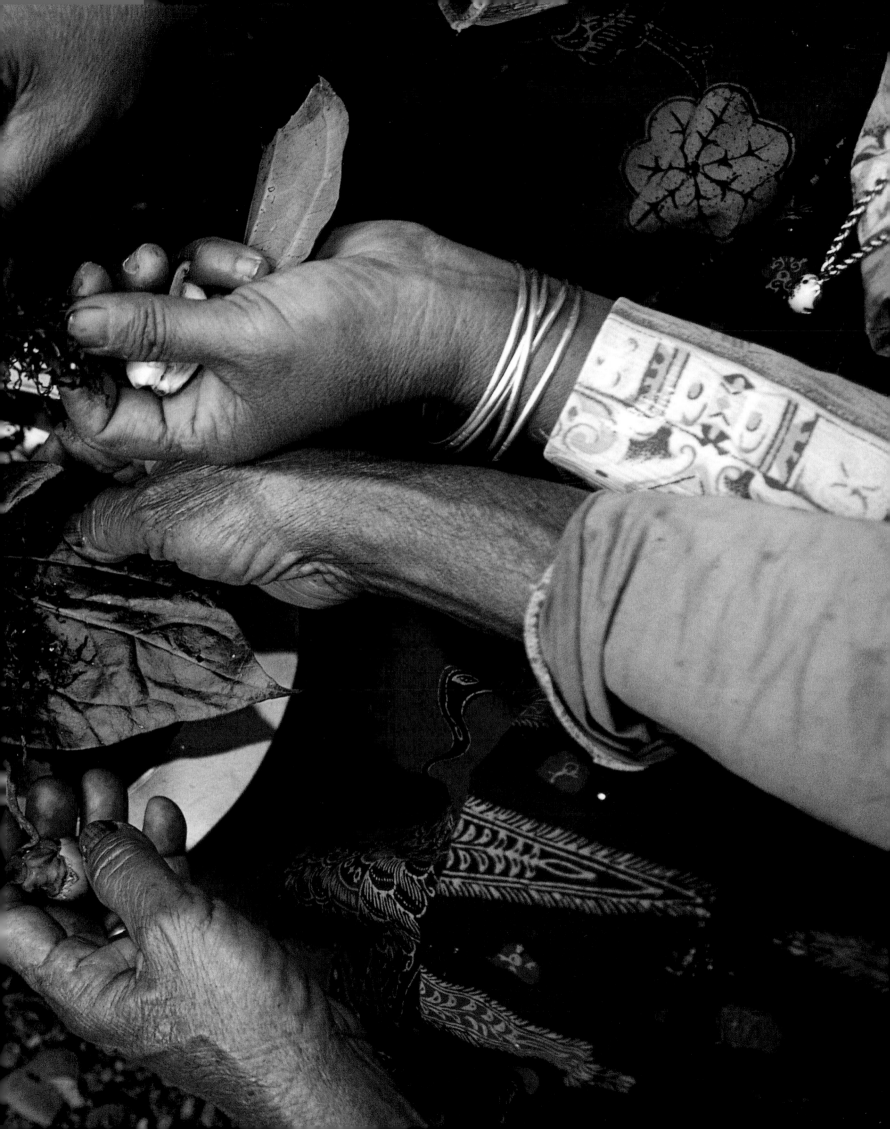

Opposite:

Breakfast for the Batak people of Lake Toba (northern Sumatra, Indonesia, 2001).

There is rice with all three daily meals. The local merchant does sell spoons but everyone prefers to eat by hand. To do without the help of one's fingers is everywhere (or almost) to act in a civilised way... but it is also to go without a pleasure as old as the world, or one could say as old as the human animal.

Following pages 44-45:

Meal time for Khampa nomads (eastern Tibet, 1991).

The child has just swallowed — using his fingers as do his parents — his bowlful of *tsampa*, a gruel of grilled barley flour which can be made into a paste with yak butter tea and which forms the basis, a little monotonous, of Tibetan food. His bowl, licked clean, has just been taken from him and he is already doing his "ablutions". To lick one's fingers after having done honour to a dish is both convenient and a mark of politeness: one has enjoyed it down to the last crumb and really wants it to be known. This gesture is long out of fashion in our puritan lands, yet our rural ancestors of the previous century still did it shamelessly, especially when water had to be spared.

Pages 46-47:

The harpist Lucia de Antoni, practising (Venetia, Italy, 2002).

The pleasures which might accompany or amplify our fingers are not only those linked to primary functions. The same happens with other "nourishment" which the hand lavishes upon us, first and foremost being that of the arts, which have become for humankind, the cultural animal, just as necessary as its bread. When one thinks about it well, there is nothing more abstract than music, which is the pure product of a body trained for a very long time in its service. There is no music that can do without either lips or hands.

Y ESTERDAY'S HUMANITY — which still stubbornly exists in some parts of the world not yet Westernised — did not conceive of beauty solely according to aesthetic criteria. To be beautiful, something had also to be good for human beings, with its benefit tried and tested. The Ancient Greeks had their own formula for bringing together these two faces of beauty: *Kallos k'Agathos*. Two faces that, in their opinion, should only make one.

Throughout the ages, the hand has been associated with finery. Jewellery, one of the most ancient arts in all cultures, has dedicated practically half of its inventions to the hand, the other half being devoted to adorning the face, and as a side-line, the foot. Though no anthropologists, the Ancient Greeks never forgot what the head, considered to be the seat of consciousness, owed to the hand and the foot. But for them, jewellery, besides being beautiful, had to hold a secret goodness for whoever wore it. Not any old hand was allowed to forge bracelets and necklaces: it required the know-how of someone initiated into the mysteries of the hidden world.

This way of seeing and of doing things still endures today. We may be tempted to view such insistence as a mere superstition. But, after all, is it superstition or simply wisdom to give credit to the harmony of things and to wish that humankind does not corrupt the fragile balance between the good and the beautiful?

Previous pages (48-49):
The bride's jewels (Chennai, South India, 2000). The hands of the bride-to-be, decorated with henna, can now "crown" her... before she offers herself to be seen, in front of everyone, by her future husband.

Opposite:
Marriage preparations among the Tuareg people of Aïr (Niger, 1999). It is the wife of the blacksmith — who is considered somewhat of a magician and guardian of secret power — who takes charge of the bride-to-be's make-up.

Following pages 52 and 53:
Making up before the Worso dance (among the Peul Bororo people, Niger, 1999). The hand helping the face: two accomplices in every act of seduction.

Opposite:

Presenting the bride-to-be's hands at a marriage in Chennai, South India, 2000.

The young girl does not yet belong to her husband but her hands, painted with henna and adorned with bracelets, speak very promisingly: beauty, wealth... and health. For the Tamil people of South India (Hindus) as for the Muslims of the Maghreb, henna is supposed to protect body and mind from attacks of the Evil One. The same goes for bracelets, also endowed with a thousand and one prophylactic qualities.

Following page:

Giving jewels to the bride (Fez, Morocco, 2000).

Of all jewels, pearls — "living" creatures, born of water — are the most sought-after. They have the gift of protecting their wearer against the "evil eye". They also assist remedies prescribed by the doctor. A sick woman is often counselled to wear all her necklaces until she is completely cured.

Page 57:

The bride's hands, painted with henna; traditional wedding in Fez (2000).

The pigment has just been applied, in intricate designs evocative of life (plants and flowers). Once dry, the brown paste falls away, leaving only a fine decorative filigree in beautiful orangey red.

Pages 58-59:

Hand-drying ritual: wedding at Fez (2000).

One finds the same ceremony, with slight variations, from the Atlantic to the Gulf of Bengal. Among the Hindus of Chennai, bride and groom present their hand to the Fire God, Agni (represented by a brazier in which flower petals and aromatics have been burnt). Here, the burner contains incense and various spices known for their medicinal properties.

Page 60:

Hands adorned for the festival: woman of the Kowa people, north-west India, 1990.

The Kowa people live in the mountains of Arunachal Pradesh State, on the frontier with Bhutan. On the morning of the festival (celebrating a nature spirit), the women adorn their hands with all their jewels, which they come to "recharge" with new protecting energy as they bring their offerings.

Page 61:

Ritual rice offering among the Apatani people (Arunachal Pradesh, 1990).

The animist Apatani people live secluded in remote valleys. On a certain date, they practice a redistribution ritual, in which the hand of the rich must feed the mouth of the poor. The offering is left in a basket dressed with leaves. The hand making the offering must wear various bracelets, each of which has a protective function: here, only the pure can give.

Opposite:

Flower-sellers at the temple gate (Chennai, South India, 2000).

The merchant aerates the petals filling his basket. It is all in the hand gesture, which is well-measured and very delicate. Not too much stirring, so as not to "tire" the flowers yet enough to revivify their beauty, which should not "die" before being scattered at the deity's feet by the faithful. It is also a way of entrusting the divinity with passing life: blossoming today, wilting tomorrow.

Following page 64:

Gujar women putting on their finery: morning of a festival in Rajasthan, 1998.

People come from hundreds of kilometres for this day of the full moon festival, which takes place on the banks of Lake Pushkar. Before leaving for the sacred bathing, the women decorate hands, feet and face with all the jewellery they possess. For their part, the men busy themselves decorating the bullock-carts which will take all the family to the banks of the lake.

Page 65:

Festive hands: Rajasthan, 1998.

This is still the autumn full moon festival. Each woman entrusts the adjusting of her finery to the hands of a relative: nothing can replace the look and gesture of another... The whole purpose is to offer the most vividly-coloured show to the moon, "feminine" wellspring of light and beauty: in a way, to repay her beauty with beauty.

Pages 66-67:

Ritual bath for the groom-to-be: Rajasthan wedding, 1998.

The women of the family show the young man their hands, just decorated with henna: in other words, purified, devoted to good and to him alone. They will then wash him, massage him, anoint him, stroke him... to make him, in turn, *beautiful* and *good*, a living present soon to be offered to his promised one.

Hands
at
Work

THE SKILLED HAND is the craftsperson's finest virtue. Though there is doubtless some natural predisposition, it comes most of all from long training. The whole of human industry was born of our ten fingers, seconded in their task, as early as fifty thousand years ago, by a whole array of tools designed to extend their efficiency and which, for the most part, have not fundamentally evolved since (yesterday, the knife was made of bone or flint, today of metal). But this — before the nineteenth century proliferation of machines powered by other energies — did not change the basic fact: *homo faber*, whether farmer, worker, craftsman or artist, needed a skilled hand.

With the new generation of industrial products, systematically distributed on a world scale (due to globalisation), consumers almost everywhere are turning away from handmade objects, considered as unprofitable for the new economy. The first price to be paid for this "progress" has of course been beauty: until our time, the useful and the beautiful always walked "hand in hand". Another price may be levied a little further down the line, when we realise that humans, on most fronts of professional life, are in the process of *losing touch* with practical know-how. One should fear this, knowing that in the West itself hundreds of trades have disappeared over the last half-century. It is evidently aberrant to oppose progress, which is one of the surest constants of humankind since it appeared on this planet. But who regulates progress? Yesterday, it was human beings themselves, after patient fumbling and adjustment. Today, it is the abstract power of money. Have we really gained anything through such a change?

Previous pages (68-69):
The potter's hands busy at their wheel: Assam, North India, 1996.

Opposite:
The garland-makers of Chennai (South India), 2000.
Sorting and braiding jasmine flowers, tasks demanding the "light touch" and mostly entrusted to men.

Following pages 72-73:
Picking jasmine (Chennai, South India, 2000). This activity is mainly reserved for women.

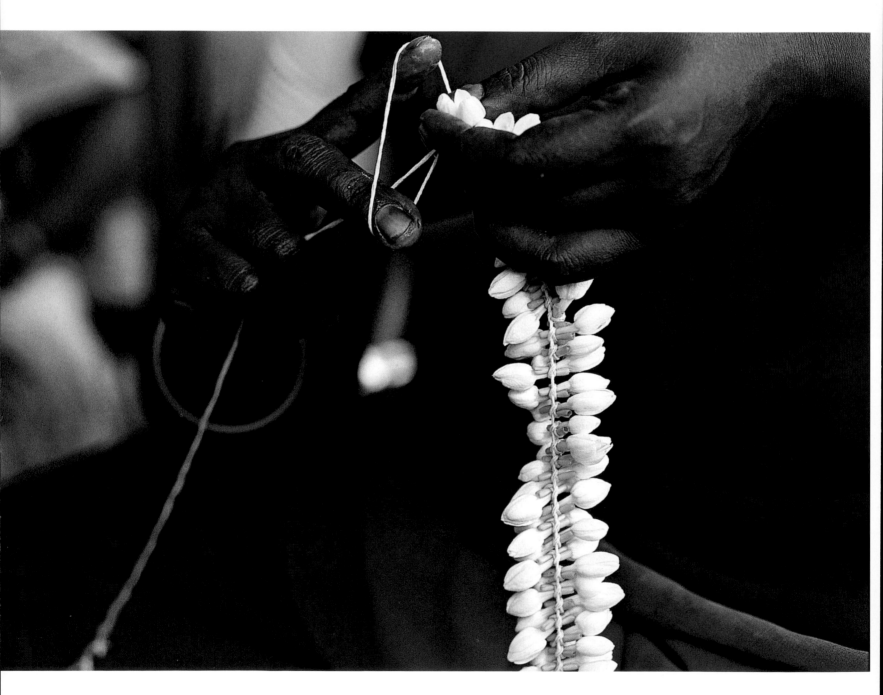

Previous pages (74 and 75):

Left: threading a jasmine garland (Chennai, South India, 2000).

The Tamil people have a high consumption of perfumed garlands, which barely last a day. They are offered to the temple gods but also used to decorate the shop, taxi or rickshaw.

Right: the hands of calligrapher Hassan Massoudy (Paris, 2002).

Someone who writes beautifully is said to have a *nice hand.*

Opposite:

Bwaba people decorating ritual masks (Burkina Faso, 1999).

The Bwaba people preserve — and bring to life — some of the most beautiful masks of Africa and some of the most impressive (some are several metres tall). Each year, the Mask Chief teaches adolescents about to enter adulthood how to tame the sacred masks — and how to decorate them for the next enthronement ceremony, which will make them responsible men. To touch the mask with one's fingertips is already to partake of its power. To restore its black, white and red colours is also to give it back its life and power. Here, as is so often the case, the hand is the prime medium of dialogue between the spirit world and that of daily life.

Following page 78:

Finishing a cloth, among the Bondo people of Orissa State (north-east India,1987).

Here it is women, and only women, who look after the making and maintenance of fabrics. This one is using an arrowhead to free threads along parts of the hem, which she will then knot into a fringe. Among the Bondo people, who are one of the most animist of India, the use of metal is restricted to the making of weapons and jewellery, the latter being considered as "protective arms" which the women never remove, for fear of their hands and face becoming prey to evil spirits.

Page 79:

The Bondo people of Orissa, putting the final touches to talismanic necklaces (1987).

Here again, only a woman's hand is allowed to make bead necklaces (in the composition of which no metal is involved). The women of the group have no fear of being seen almost naked by strangers, as long as their faces, hands and chests are decorated with enough protective necklaces and bracelets.

Opposite:
Fishing net on the Brahmaputra (Assam, 1996).

The net is nothing without the skill of the hand which fashions it, mends it, casts it and hauls it in. Experienced fishers know that, all said and done, the net is nothing other than the hand's accomplishment.

Following page 82:
The basket-weavers of Szu-Chu'an (south-west China, 1991).

This is one of the most important centres for bamboo. From the young shoots, cut into strips, can be made baskets, winnows, fish-pots, food racks... Whereas pottery is no older than ten thousand years, basket work is probably as old as humanity, which must have made its first containers much as birds make their nests. This is yet another trade where "all is in the hand" and to which many traditions attribute a sacred character. The symbolic criss-crossing of horizontal and vertical energies (found in the sign of the cross well before Christianity) depict, for the basket-maker as for the weaver, a summary of the world.

Page 83:
Winnowing grain in Rajasthan (1998).

To finish separating chaff from grain, one can either use the traditional winnow (a basket shaken into the wind, which carries away the chaff, the grain falling to earth) or else, when there is no wind, vigorously turn the mixture of grain and impurity by hand in a circular container... taking advantage of the centrifugal force, which whisks the chaff, which is lighter, out of the container.

Here, a woman is in charge of this task. It is a whole art acquiring the right hand movement: one which lets the minimum amount of grain escape from the container.

Page 84:
Harvesting cinnamon in Sumatra (2001). This work is entrusted to men, the women then taking care of the sorting and drying.

Page 85:
Pruning the vines at Scarnafigi (Piedmont, 2002). Wine-grower's proverb, "Your mouth will have good wine if your hand has done good pruning."

Page 86:
Sheep-shearing in the Kongpo valley (south-east Tibet), 1995. Shears, hardly modernised, are an invention of the Bronze Age.

Page 87:
Spinning wool in the Kongpo valley (1995). The same rudimentary distaff is still in use in Europe, in the Maramur region (Romanian Carpathians).

Cooking in the tent, nomads of Kham (eastern Tibet, 1991).

The cook is stirring the seasonal dish: a soup of aquatic plants gathered in the high-altitude marshes. In most societies — and until recently in our own — it was only women who looked after the tasks of nourishing the family. This tradition still continues, even in so-called evolved societies. Food critics give particular acclaim to "female cooking", which has the reputation of being more straightforward and more natural. It is known that the best restaurants in Lyons, the French capital of good food, were run by generations of "mothers", who only handed down their secret personal touch to their daughters.

Following page 90:

Preparing coconut milk on the eve of a marriage (Sumatra, Indonesia, 2000).

Hand-pressed milk is thought to be the best. It is made by crushing the pulp of the fruit in a cloth. Both milk and pulp residue will later be used to make *galamaï*, wedding cakes.

These days, it is a luxury to do "by hand" what machines can accomplish. As such, it is also often an activity that is gradually disappearing, even though connoisseurs decry the loss of quality. It is well known that comfort, in its most modern definition and however much needed, does not always enrich the quality of life.

Page 91:

Crushing peppers for a village festival (Sumatra, 2001).

Yet another task for women, even though it requires a strong hand. Here they are crushed to a paste on a block of basalt.

Pages 92-93:

Shaping cob loaves at Signols, Upper Susa Valley (Piedmont, Italy, 2002).

Having been kneaded, the risen dough is then shaped. These two women work at home yet still prepare the bread for the entire village. Once ready, the cob loaves will be taken to the public oven, in the square.

One forgets that bread, which was the staple food of half the world's population for many centuries, is a pure product of the hand. Almost everywhere machines have taken over... more to the satisfaction of industry than the consumer.

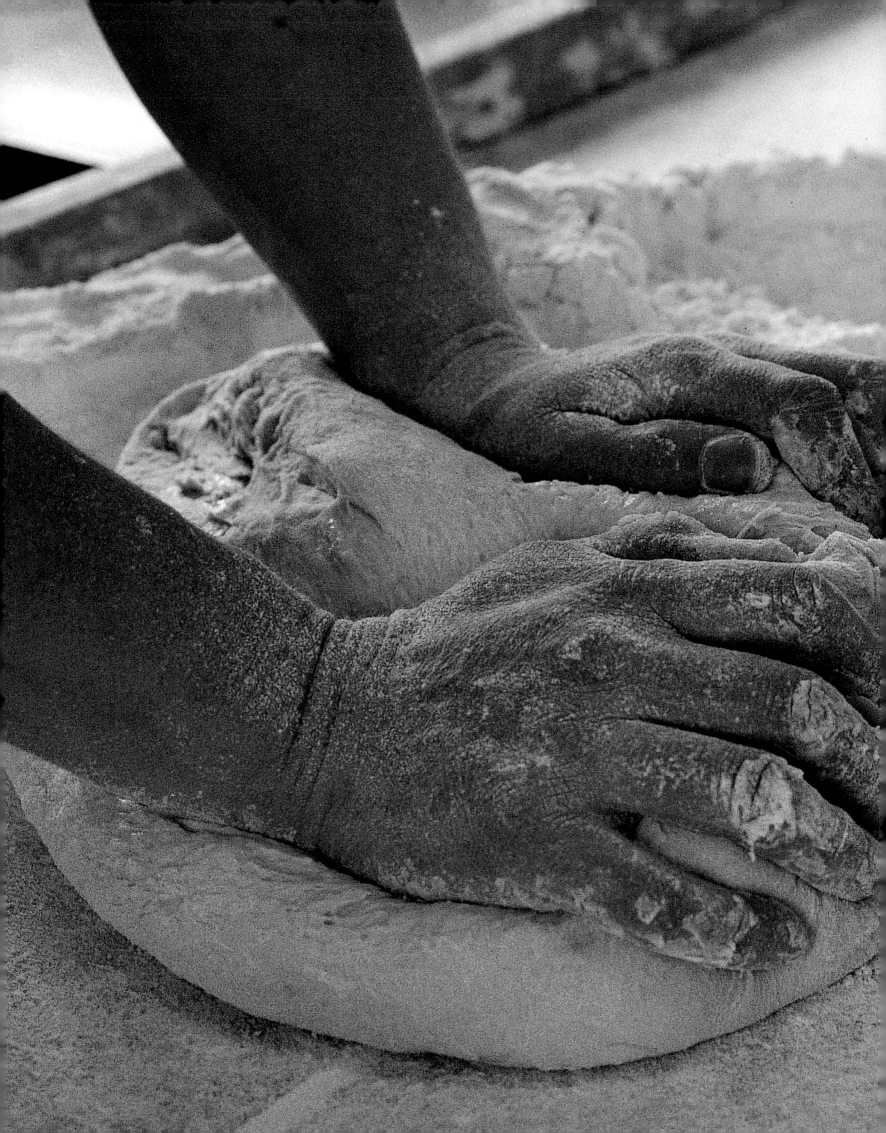

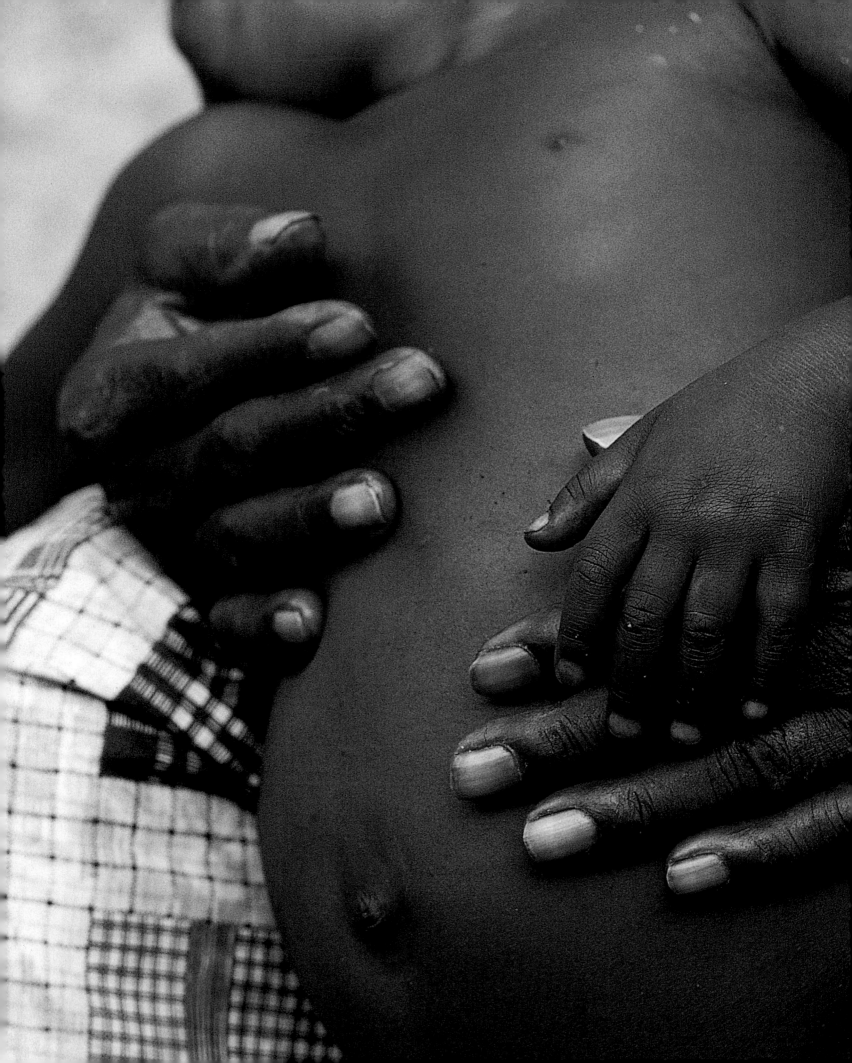

Hands
of
the
Heart

It is the hand which brings humanity the added pleasure and beauty its frustrated consciousness feels to be missing. The hand provides the tool enabling things — almost anything — to be made. It creates art, which conjures up the enigmatic forces of creation before rivalling them. To the mouth, it brings the bread and water of life, while nonetheless competing with it to express its own *tongue*, as shown by Boris Cyrulnik. Could the grammar of hand gestures ever be described exhaustively, with its varied declensions, its ambiguities and the full spectrum of its vocabulary?

As photographers with a geographers' curiosity that compelled us to travel among ethnic groups whose tongues we did not speak — despite the long preparation that is required before any journey, it is true — we learned that we would find it hard to practice our trade were it not for hand language. It is a sort of *Volapük*, a universal language with some amusing exceptions to its universality (Greeks who appear to say yes when they are actually saying no!). We caught this language in action everywhere, without looking for it. The attitude of anyone faced with a photographer seeking approbation before framing the shot almost invariably translates itself by a hand gesture, which is either eloquent in itself or which emphasises a facial expression that says it all.

The hand does not speak only in response. We have seen it everywhere talking in its own right, expressing all: acceptance and refusal, tenderness and disdain, distrust and curiosity, protection and threat, modesty and seduction, wariness and confidence and complicity or distance. The list is far from being exhaustive, and each gesture instantly delivers its whole range of restrictions, emphases, qualifiers or *double entendres*. Hence a few misunderstandings, of course. Typical of any language: one says something, then contradicts oneself.

Impassivity, so highly commended by the puritanical education of yesteryear, is not really favoured by humankind, as we shall see here, in pictures.

Previous pages (94-95):
Child on the knees of his grandfather in a village of Burkina Faso (1999). Affection and protection: this message needs no words.

Opposite:
Mother with child, Peul Bororo people of Niger (1984). The little boy's finger learnt to speak before his mouth did.

Opposite:

In a story-teller's house: Kongpo, south-east Tibet, 1995.

The boy is listening to frightening tales. They are often atrocious — somewhat like the Grimm stories — nevertheless young souls need to learn that evil does exist and that life is a hard struggle.

Here the dominant legends are those portraying the famous "women poisoners", some of the area's celebrities (rumour has it some of them are still active today). In order to protect their domain from the idle curiosity of certain travellers, these formidable magicians made poisons of a rare subtlety: someone who had imbibed them inadvertently while staying in this fiercely-guarded area might not suffer the effects for some days, some weeks or even some months after having left... and would die without being able to identify the hand that dealt death's blow.

On the shoulder of he who listens with staring eyes is placed the protective hand of his elder brother, who has heard even worse tales but judges the moment timely to intervene. The simple pressure of his fingers recalls his message: "I am there, don't be afraid, just listen..."

Opposite:

In the tent of nomads of Amdo, north-east Tibet, 1992.

The Golok nomads camp in yak-hair tents, on the high frozen plateaus of Amdo, in the far north-east of Tibet, not far from the vast Kokonor lake. This is doubtless one of the least visited areas of Central Asia and one in which, twenty-five years ago, none of the inhabitants would have ever seen a Westerner. The hand and face tell it all: astonishment... in which fear is already giving way to curiosity.

Following page 102:

Young Khampa girl in a village of the Upper Brahmaputra (Kongpo), south-east Tibet, 1996.

The hand and the look in eloquent contradiction: the fingers in the mouth give the impression of being overwhelmed by worry... while the eye betrays a wanting to know more. Thus warned, it is up to the stranger to decide on the best approach.

Page 103:

Shepherd of the Maramurian mountains, Romanian Carpathians, 1994.

Mouth and index finger are agreed: perplexity in face of the unknown. Yet the eyes, not that far from a smile, already give the intruder a good welcome. Throughout the world, one thing is constant: the shepherd, who has nothing or barely anything, belongs to a class of people ready to give all they have. They have chosen the solitary life but a meeting is always something to celebrate.

Page 104:

A young boy, caught by surprise in a side street of the In-Gall oasis (Nigeria, 1986).

This region, near Agades, is quite visited. Has he never seen a stranger before (the ostrich also hides its head so as not to see what scares it)? Or else it could be a case of the old game of love and fear, which all the world's children like to play among themselves and with others, to seek reassurance: "tell me that you love me too and that I'm wrong to be afraid..."

Page 105:

Adolescent at a time of doubt: in a school of eastern Mauritania, 1999.

He is still a child and so can allow himself to make this gesture of placing fingers in front of mouth, part of the international vocabulary of childhood acknowledged. To be deciphered: what the glance is on the look-out for, what the mouth suggests and what the hand holds. We are told that he is the most timid of the class. We understand: "Don't rush me... I'm giving you this quarter-smile... I daren't say more than that." Words, however, struggle to interpret properly the complexity of his message. It would take sentence upon sentence and even then they would never attain such precision.

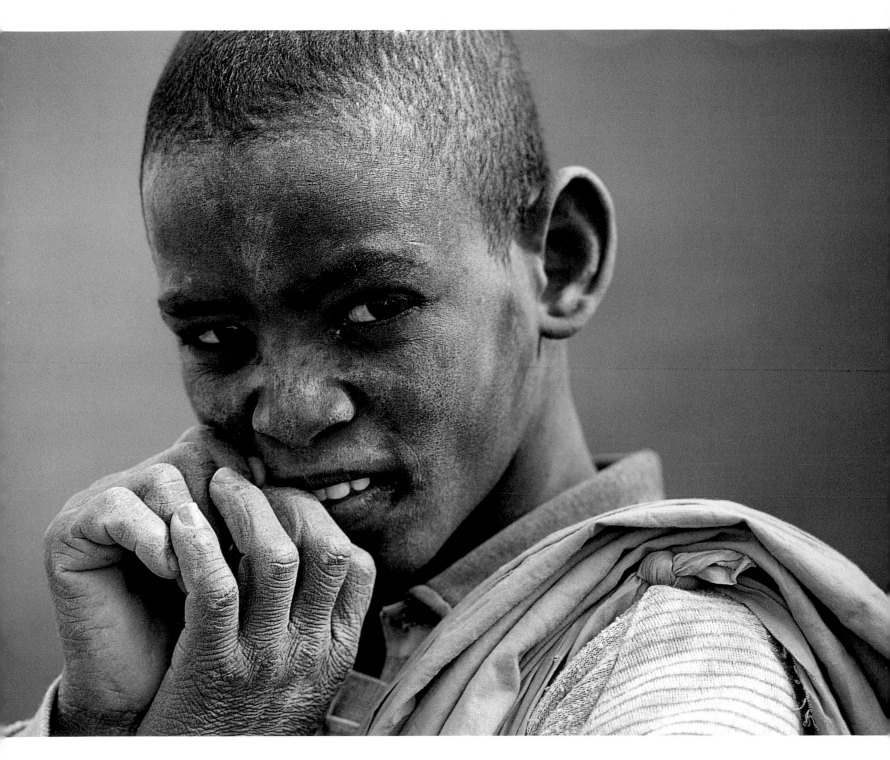

Opposite:
Brahmin taking advantage of the cool in front of the temple: Pushkar, Rajasthan, 1997.

He definitely means NO! But too late: we had just taken him by surprise one second earlier... the finger on the shutter button spoke whereas our lips contradicted its action and mumbled our excuses. Not fooled, his face reflects what, according to him, we deserve: disgust and pity.

Following page 108:
Young girl, eastern Mauritanian oasis, 1999.

Hands resting on lips: according to the gesture they can signify, in turn, astonishment, complicity, silence... Dominant here is surprised modesty, with all its usual range of nuances — the ones linguists call "the unspoken".

Page 109:
Modesty is sometimes a ploy: in this case, we found out that she wanted to be photographed. The eye should have warned us.

Page 110:
Rabari woman on the threshold of her house: Gujarat, north-west India, 1999.

The Rabari people, who are semi-nomadic, spending part of their year on the road, are thought to be the ancestors of our gypsies. A mystery to be investigated: is biting one's nails really a remedy for worry?

Page 111:
Bondo woman, Orissa State, north-east India, 1986.

The animist Bondo people live today much as people did in the early Metal Ages. Isolated from the world, they are by nature reserved yet know how to give a hearty welcome to the traveller who ventures as far as their land. It is a fine gesture which expresses this; one of modesty and complicity.

Pages 112 and 113:
Two forms of complicity...

Left: two young women of the Bhil people (southern Rajasthan, 1988). To hide oneself and show oneself are the two obligatory phases of seduction. It is a little comedy made easier by feeling one has the support of a friend, an accomplice without which, one may think, the hand would not risk such impertinence...

Right: two betel chewers at chatting time (the Minangkabao people of Sumatra, 2000). The two index fingers touching each other need no interpreting: "You and I, we make a pair..."

Pages 114-115:
In a Qur'an school of Minangkabao (Sumatra), 2001. The hands are often more talkative than the lips, at the time of pronouncing friendship.

106

Hands
of
Ritual

HUMANS OF PREHISTORICAL TIMES attempted to tame Death, as we are reminded by Boris Cyrulnik, and drew their hands on cave walls to assert their presence in the world. They did so not just to show they were there but to persuade others — and themselves too — that, though they may be submitted perforce to the mysterious Will that governs beings and things, they must nevertheless impose another will on those beings and things: their own. This (later to be called *freedom*) was perhaps a dangerous illusion and one that they shouldered by trying to win the good graces of the obscure powers that manifested their Will above their heads. In other words, they tried to fit their own choices within a ritual framework, so that they could get their own way without ruining the harmony they felt at work around them.

It is always easy to mock a ritual by measuring its value by the only yardstick we know, that of raw efficiency. On those sorts of grounds, the doctor will forever ridicule the shaman. But ritual cares little for quantifiable success; the order it dreams of instituting is above all qualitative and does not make any other claim than to be attuned to the harmony of the great All. Whatever the era or location, ritual may end up being dismissed or caricatured as superstition but this in no way invalidates its basic premise. The hand of ritual only aims to impose upon humanity the measure of a certain *quality* of existence, through controlling the gestures of a hand that makes and builds things, but which also has the power to destroy them.

Previous pages (116-117):
Distributing 'long-life' pills (eastern Tibet, 1992).
Every year, the monks of Katok monastery, in Kham, prepare this magic medicine for the pilgrims who go there in their thousands. These hands are doubtlessly stretched out through credulity (to believe in the impossible is a constant human element)... but also, let us be careful of this, through wanting to respect a certain measure of life codified by Buddhist wisdom.

Opposite:
Ritual 'Cham' dance in Tsasa monastery (eastern Tibet, 1992).
The young man leading the ceremony is brandishing the sacred thunderbolt (a piece of wood, dyed red), supposed to channel good energies received by the hand reaching to the heavens.

119

Page 120:
Looking after the butter-lamps at Shalu monastery (eastern Tibet, 1995). The monk on watch always keeps a burette of melted yak butter in his hand to bring the flame back to life: no lamp should ever go out.

Page 121:
Night time celebration of Diwali (Festival of Light) on the banks of Lake Pushkar (Rajasthan, 1998). This is the night upon which the faithful seek the favours of Lakshmi, Goddess of Light, of Fortune... and of Business (this festival marks the start of the financial year). Lakshmi will be present throughout the year, wherever the flame has been carried.

Pages 122-123:
A *sadhu* (ascetic) taking his ritual bath on the banks of Lake Pushkar, India (1998). The hand washed in the waters of the sacred lake is empowered to purify all.

Page 124:
Vishnuite *sadhu* (Lake Pushkar, India, 1998). The holy man dedicates every minute of his life to prayer. His rosary must never leave his hand.

Preceding page 125:
A *sadhu* at the hour of lustral splashing (Lake Pushkar, 1998). Once purified, the hand can deliver its virtues to each part of the body.

Opposite:
Blessing of the prayer leader (Ajmer Mosque, Rajasthan, 1998). The believer brings a few small delicacies as an offering to the "master", whose hand transmits to the visitors the blessings he has received from heaven.

Following pages 128 and 129:
Man and woman praying (Ajmer Mosque, Rajasthan, 1998). Their palms must be turned towards the heavens, as a sign of their "availability" (*Islam*).

Page 130:
Session of sponsored prayer (Ajmer Mosque, Rajasthan, 1998). The noble people gathered here are pious but poor. Each one of them has been commissioned by someone rich who cannot find the time to think of heaven and so has given him the task of praying for him. With each prayer, the hand counts a grain, which the "prayer-maker" places before himself on a pile which comprises the day's blessings. For each grain, a small coin will be received.

Page 131:
Processing the Urs (Ajmer Mosque, Rajasthan, 1968). This day's festival marks the holy Sufi buried in the sanctuary. The pilgrims push to touch the lintel of the "Gate of Paradise".

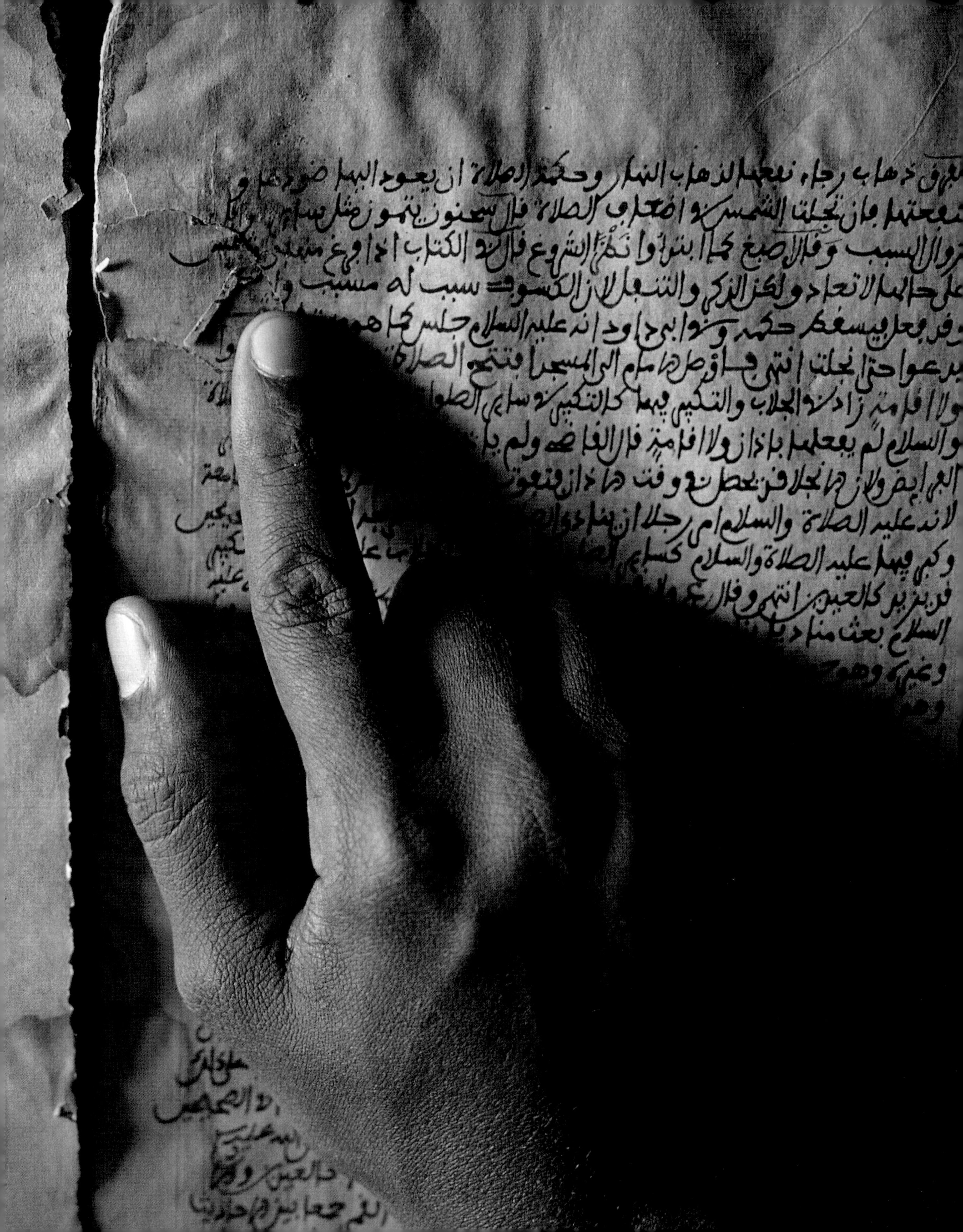

Page 132:
Reading the Qur'an in the Walata Mosque (southern Mauritania, 1999). The finger resting on the text is not a simple marker. It speaks of the attachment of the person reciting to the word of God.

Preceding page 133:
In the library-tent of nomads of the Tichitt region (eastern Mauritania, 1999). It is the women here who are in charge of looking after the books: preserving them, putting them in order and lending them to those who ask. Their hands are reputed to be "pleasant for God".

Opposite:
The hand protecting the prayer (monk on pilgrimage to Mount Kailash, western Tibet, 1995). Praying comes down to associating the three 'thresholds' of the soul: the eye which deciphers the prayer, the mouth which chants and the hands which turn the volume's pages and keep account of the time given to heaven.

Following page 136:
Hands at prayer... A woman on pilgrimage in the streets of Ahmedabad (Gujarat, north-west India, 1986).

Page 137:
A monk, turning the pages of a prayer book (Sakya monastery, central Tibet, 1995). There was no book, be it *volumen* or *codex*, that was not first fashioned by hand.

Page 138:
A shaman looking into the future (among the Tagin people of Arunachal Pradesh, north-west India, 1996). The Tagin people, who belong to the Tibeto-Burmese ethnic group, practise animism. Just like the augurers of ancient Rome, the diviner-priest needs "the eye and the hand". On the festival of Si-donji, which marks the beginning of a seasonal cycle, he rips apart a chicken liver with his own hands and "reads" in it the destiny promised for the village for the year to come.

Page 139:
A contortionist *sadhu*: the Parasuram-Khund pilgrimage (Arunachal Pradesh, 1996). As Parasuram had decapitated his mother on his father's orders, the axe-blade remained stuck to his hand. Coming to the spot traditionally thought to be the source of the Brahmaputra, he dips his hand in the water and is freed. The "pure" hand holds the power to submit the entire body to its law, as this *sadhu* reminds us, by dislocating the joints of his arms with his own hands and re-setting them at will.

Pages 140-141:
Ritual rice offering: marriage ceremony in Minangkabao (western Sumatra, 2000).

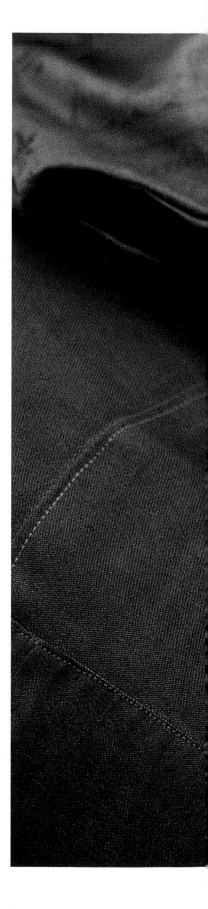

By
Hand...

IF, AS ANTHROPOLOGISTS ASSURE US, the hand has made humans what they are, it is because they entrusted it very early on with the mission of fulfilling their dreams; all their dreams. Nearly everything we do is done by our hands: cooking and lovemaking, industry and art, war and prayer. The good and the bad, both.

The hand makes our desires a reality and makes our inventions take shape. It is the hand again that expresses our sentiments and does half of our "talking". It is the hand, yet again, which shows the solidarity without which men and women would not be the social animals known as "humans".

Machines may become able to replace the hand in many tasks but they will find it hard to supersede. And should they do so, it would not be good news, as humankind might lose its humanity. This is a loss one cannot wish for, even if the hand is not always put to good use.

Previous pages (142-143):
Yakay dance during the Worso festival, among the Peul Bororo people (Niger, 1986).
Young male candidates for marriage are dressed up to seduce the girls attending their dance. The face is made to stand out... as well as the hands, for it is through them that woman gains pleasure and protection.

Opposite:
Khampa woman taking tea (eastern Tibet, 1991). Without the hand which gives food and drink, humans beings would be obliged to stoop to nourish themselves.

Following page 146:
The hand of labour... The agricultural worker only has to show his palm to disclose all that his existence owes to his hand (Piedmont, Italy, 2002).

Page 147:
A hunter in his costume, during the Imst carnival (Tyrol, Austria, 1992). People of the high valleys are happy to claim the status that was theirs at the dawn of time: trackers of game. Through the millennia, the sense of smell has diminished, yet this hand which protects the volatile scent of a freshly-picked juniper spray still dreams of a world in which all could be known and recognised by its odour.

Page 148:
Love-story on the grass: in a Sumatran village, Indonesia (2000). To take another's hand makes a pact which needs no words.

Page 149:
A halt for the nomads of the Mauritanian desert (1999). The nights are cold: everyone comes to "wake their hands up" by the fire. "Nothing down here can be done by sleeping hands," reminds a proverb dear to all the desert people.

Preceding pages 150 and 151:
Two street scenes during the Pushkar pilgrimage (Rajasthan, India, 1998).
Left: a *sadhu* showing his marks of "saintliness" (the atrophied leg is not due to some illness but to ascetic practices of immobility). An American tourist scolded us for our "insensitivity" when he saw us take this photo... but this was to the great dismay of the subject, who saw it, on the contrary, as a mark of our respect and interest! As for the woman passing by, she does not hesitate. As she cannot make gifts to the holy man, who refuses offerings, she stretches out a hand to feed the parrot.
Right: a young pilgrim, made up as Hanuman (the Monkey God), practising ritual begging... the money in his hand is not something shameful but rather something to be proud of.

Opposite:
Enthronement of *penghulu* (village chief): western Sumatra, Indonesia, 2001. The chief's staff gives distinction to a "fine hand": strong and beneficent.

Following pages 154 and 155:
Speech by a *penghulu* of the Minangkabao people of western Sumatra (2001). The chief is consulted regularly concerning the *adat* (code of conduct of which he is guardian). As the orators of ancient Rome taught, skilled eloquence must know how to make a hand "speak".

Pages 156-157:
Women leaving the mosque (western Sumatra, 2001). Those who *give* their hand give all — and in so doing make the other their ally.

Page 158:
Reciting the Qur'an (southern Mauritania, 1999). The hand laid on the text marks its allegiance to the divine word.

Page 159:
The story-teller's hand: Tuareg people of Tassili (southern Algeria, 1984). The fingers drawing in the sand "comment on" the speech: the hand also has the power to tell of life.

158

159

The authors
would like to thank all the hands which speak in this book
and in particular those of
Hassan Massoudy, Nando Ballario, Lucia De Antoni, Yakouba Bondé,
Putri Bulgish Shofwan, Cristina Mandelli, Hassan of the Kassawa Peul people,
Jothi Sankar, Melika, Severino Carena, Guy Baoumo, Jika of the Djamparem Peul people,
Rang Lal, Ravikant Sharma, Ayaz Maharaj, Mohamedon Ould Baba,
Anani Abdallah, Nabouya Sidi,
Datuk Ankayo Syaharyal Penghulu Suku Sikumbang,
Amayed.
As well as the hands belonging to
the women of the Rousset families of Signoles; the women of Mesjid Asasi;
the *sadhus* of Pushkar and Parasuram Khund;
not to mention all the anonymous hands belonging to artists, craftspeople
or simple passers-by,
pilgrims or shamans, nomads or farmers, highlanders or fishers,
children or old people
without which this book
could not have been.

This work,
created under the guidance of
Jean-Pierre Sicre
from the original layout
of Alain Meylan
was printed
in Segrate, Italy, by Grafiche Milani.

Photo-engraving by
Grafotitoli of Sesto San Giovanni.
Bound by Grafiche Milani in Segrate.